What Men Should Know About Women

ERICA M. LOBERG

CHIPMUNKA CLASSICS

CHIPMUNKA CLASSICS

All rights reserved, no part of this publication may be reproduced by any means, electronic, mechanical photocopying, documentary, film or in any other format without prior written permission of the publisher.

Published by
Chipmunkapublishing
United Kingdom

http://www. chipmunkaclassics.co.uk

Copyright © Erica M. Loberg 2015

ISBN   978-1-78382-204-1

Poetry is a stiff mind
And a hard drink
-eml

CHAPTER ONE: THE SELF

A WARRIOR

Life is hard when you look back at it
And don't know how to look forward to it
When the present isn't where you want it to be.

Life is going to throw itself at you
Give you balls you might be able to dodge
Waves you might be able to break.

Might
Or not.

What matters is you keep moving forward
Keep your head held high
Even when it weighs itself
On your fragile shoulders.

Life is called life for a reason.

You meet the good with the bad
The raw with the lies
The light with the dark

The dichotomy of the ebb and flow of life
Will continue to meet you
Push you.

And make you a warrior.

A DOG SWIMMING IN MUD

Am I self-destructive. Absolutely.
Where does the destruction find itself.

Why do I allow the harsh, the real, the unbroken,
the bleep on the horizon
Be flattened
Like a penny
On a railroad.

Buried beneath the surface is a smothered power.

How do I search it out?

Like a dog scurries for a bone in the mud.

LOSING A LOVED ONE, LOSING LOVE, LOSING LOGIC

When you lose the old self
You find the new self

It trickles in
In small ways

You go back to your yoga class
You call people you haven't spoken to in awhile

You try to find balance
In chaos

And in that transition
There's a spice of
Fun

Change is hard
But change is good

Especially when you see
The changes

And find yourself

Again.

MIND GAMES WITH YOURSELF

I want out but can't get out
I want in but shouldn't stay in

I want me
When I still want you

I guess I don't know what I want
Or don't know how to handle it.

NOTE TO SELF

Shit shit
I can't find my pot..

Opened drawers
Spots around the place
Corners of a windowsill?
Rummaging through cabinets
Under the sink
In the bathroom
Where where

Mother Teresa

I found it.

Desk drawer right side next to your stapler.

Note to self.

SIMPLY ENERGY

Energy thrusts itself
Into the madness of madness

Whatever your madness is
It grows
It pulls
It's quiet beneath the
Fake magic
Then jumps out
Screams
And makes a sting

And you realize
Energy
Is your only friend
Your being
Your pride
Your tears
Your love
Your human existence
Yourself

Energy lives
In
Within
As
And will always be

Simply
Energy

JUST ME

I'm nearing 40
And lost my man
Lost my person
Lost my tiny future

And now I go to the gynecologist
And he asks me about
Freezing my eggs

And I'm so confused
I'm so amazed
I'm so bewildered
I'm so lost
I'm so angry
I'm so not beloved

I'm just with myself

Just me.

OK then.

AND YOU ARE ALONE AGAIN

And you are alone again
Again
Again
In the mist of love
You shout out
And get depleted
You cry out
And get shut down

Being real
Becomes a source
Of hate
A reason to reframe
Language.

It's so hard
The heartbreak
The sadness
The lost dreams
The lost soul
That hopefully
Finds
New wonder
New wants
No love
New truth
Now

SOMETHING

SEEING YOURSELF OUTSIDE OF YOURSELF

Sometimes we actually do have a choice

Not to cry

And when that moment sits on the brink of your tearful blink
Stop. Take in a breath
And allow yourself to
Break

A break away from
The tears
And thoughts
That bleed
Those tears

And sit up tall
Take a look around your existence

The books on your shelf
The bedspread you selected
The pictures on you your walls
The towels in your bathroom

Take a good surveillance
Of yourself
Reflected in the self that

Sits here now.

Tears never get dissolved
Cause they never fall from the rim of your lid
Cause you're a new you

A you that encompasses
The old self
Sprinkled throughout
Your living breathing space

Sometimes it takes a good look around
To see yourself

Outside of yourself.

AS WE DOUBT

The uncertainty
Hits below the belt
Under the surface
Of yourself

Whether it's your relationship
Or your professional life
However it unfolds

It's the uncertainties of the plot of
Your life

That makes us move forward
As we doubt.

I WONDER

Sometimes I wonder
When will I
Not be happy
Or God forbid
Content.

Sometimes I wonder
If I'll just be
Okay.

With
Whatever brought me here
And kept me here.

And holds on so tight
That's I can't release myself

From me.

HAIRFULL

Back when I had hair
I had hairfull
Confidence.

Back when I had you
I had hairfull
Sex.

Back when I had a job
I had hairfull
Days.

Now that I'm
Without
All 3
I have hair holding onto…
Something
I have to find

To keep it.

SUCKELING THE DARK TIT

Stop the madness
Of depression
Simmering in my
Bones
And taking over
My home.

Where I am
Alone
Suckling off the tit of
Dark sadness

With no stop
To the

Madness.

THANK GOD IT'S TIME

I'm close to the end

The end of no ends
Of dark nonsense
Of nothingness
Without any hope
Or productive path
Or desire to
Become what you are
What you need to be
To be alive
To be you
The person sitting here now
Inside the limbs of your creation.

Yeah, I'm a person
Ready to live
To tell
To think
To be.

So find a way for the rest of
To go.

NO MORE

I'm stuck
I'm not lost
I'm not
Not aware
I'm a bubbling stream.

My blood flows through my body
Or down my arm
Or penetrates the
Foot.

My blood slips down my vein like
A lava stream.

And now there are some bubbles
On the top of the
Blood stream.

And I'm floating down the stream
In a bubble.

But I don't want to be in the bubble
Much more

No more.

IT

There's a point when it

Begs your strength to

Come back.

Be who you are.
And release yourself from your current surroundings.

You break out

You breathe hard

You stand tall.

The web of uncertainty ends

And the era of champion sets in.

And it's great.

It's not worth all the bullshit you've been through to get there

But

It's worth a moment of

FUCK YEAH!

DESPERATION DISSECTED IN SILK SHEETS

I wonder why
Celebrities are so thin...
Desperation to succeed
Maintain their paparazzi fans
Acquire or sustain their 8000 thread sheets
Deep-seated desperation
Breeds success
In the pursuit of physical fitness
The layers beneath remain
Unknown.
Sad.
Social pressure builds an exterior
And the collapse of the inner and outer self
The brain and the body
Live alone.
The disconnection
Endures solitude
Fooled into being happy
Sleeping in silk sheets.
Is that why rich people claim
To be unhappy
Maybe there is some truth
To the obvious.
Dissected desperation
Blocked my friends
Waking up to flowers by the bed
Or a cat
On your pillow
Or the cotton remnants deep in the pillow

To recall the immediate gratification of last nights
remnants of sex

A body beside the space.

PLEASE

Please please please find a way to not return to that old decrepit self

That old decrepit self that breaths beneath the surface of the wannbe real self
That calls to itself, cries with itself

And hopes somehow it will suck the bad into the ground
And find a way to make flowers
Not shit infested mushrooms from my cats crap in my plant
To a plentiful new spring home
Where all the dark that I endure
Finds itself a wild plant

For someone to realize

As bad as it is
The shit that is meshed into the ground
Will always be there
Waiting to be watered

And you can only pray you've planted other
Flowers
In the mirage of life

And when those cloudy flowers breathe up into the air
You already have a forest of fresh and new pedals to eat

And breath up into a nose that is slowly finding it's way toward

No bullshit.

STERILE JUICE

That's what you call it

Sterile juice

When you're dead inside
And that death becomes a juice
That kills all the other juices

That keep us alive.

INDEED

Sometimes you feel things so deep
That the tears remind you that your heart
Bleeds
And your soul
Screams
Softly.

I stare out my window
And watch the cars pass
Los Angeles Blvd.
And wonder
When the tears will dry
When will the laugher
Return.

Where do you return to?
When you don't know where you're at?

But you do
The sound whispers
The heart bleeds
You get a visual
Of the human condition
And it makes you shudder
And it makes you sing.

And you let the tears dry
On your face
And welcome a new smile and say

Yup. I'm great.
Indeed

AN OUT DOOR IDEA

Principle has no duties, no liability, no obligations
It's just this happy outdoor idea
That sounds like
I'm doing it better
Or at trying to

When principle is not at work

Among the people.
Among the Wall Street sharks.
Among the Internet snakes.
The industry idiots.
The merchant thirsty lawyers.

Principle is a word that will lose itself
Lose its right
Lose everything it's about

Cause no one is ready to stand for it.

WHAT'S RIGHT, AND WHAT'S WRONG, FOR YOU.

It's hard to know what to do
When you know what to do
But you can't seem to
Do it.

Sometimes we suffocate ourselves
With our own
Selves

And the strength to move forward and make decisions
Are lost

In my tendencies?
In my weakness?
In my love for where I am now?

But when you don't love it
And don't know any better
Cause you find change
Hard

You are left with
Yourself

Tell yourself
You can do it
Whatever it is
Find a new job

Find a mate
Fix your car
Lose the pile of papers on your desk.

There is so much to win
When we lose

What keeps us back?

IT'S NOT THAT EASY

I know who I am
Deep inside.

Yet always on the surface
Is the other self.

I feel that deep self inside
Peeping out through the clouds
Of my outdoor self

Of my existence.

I know it's there
Yet I choose to ignore it.

I walk through my life
Not in my life.

Cause if I walked
In my life
I'm forced to deal
With all the pain, rubbish, tarnish

That makes me a flawed human.

I want to walk in my life
Not through it.

But, it's not that easy.

THE DEMON

Inside and beside
The heart of me

Is the demon.

The do gooder
Pumps out blood

To survive.

And the demon
Can fang itself onto that
Fresh blood.

And your body either
Fights it
Dispels it

Or becomes it.

BAKED

Baked
Stoned
I'm going home

Tonight was long
We hit the bong

Walking home
I'm not alone

The buzz sits still
Swirling in
My gills.

CHAPTER TWO: THE BODY

THE INCH OF THE ANKLE BONE

The protruding inch of my anklebone
The elbow knob
My wrist bump
Vertebrae back bone
The surface of my hipbone
Barely hitting the seams of my skirt
The ball like formation of my shoulder
That accents my skinny arm and
The three horizontal sheets of linear flat bones
Across my chest.

Are the points of I'm doing all right.

I'M TIRED OF TAKING MY PILLS

I'm tired of taking pills.
I'm not just tired of it
I'm over it.

I'm tired of wondering if I'd be better off
Without them.

So what if hypomania is a crime
To the uneducated public.

I'm tired of taking my pills.

But I do
I continue to do
Since the day I was told to.

When I worked in a psych ward
No one ever took their meds
They had to go before a judge to legally make them take them.

And I have the choice
And although I don't want to
I do.

ZOLOFT AND IN BETWEEN

I think I'm losing
My hair.

Yeah.

Like in between in between in between
That unbeaten

It's unmustering of
Attention.

Is it a sign of
Depression?

Or of
The anti depressant
I'm shoveling in.

Am I depressed longer
And more worse
Then before
Five years
Ago?

Why is my hair
Thinned
To
Thinner
Thinned out.
Of some slit hair.

Glancing the scalp when you hairdry
Or when it's a day old
And greased against your
Balding head
You notice it.

So is it the depression or
The stress

The you fucked someone in front of me?

HOW MANY TIMES

How many times am I going to squeeze my roll of fat
Sitting happily
Over the rim of my underwear

When will it be okay

That it will never be

Gone.

I poke at my fat
Here and there

Often.

Especially when I sit on the toilet
Everyone has to do it
Sit down
Pull down their clothes and

There it is

That roll of fat
Smiling on the rim of your thighs.

Hello, how are you? I'm still here!

Yup! Thanks!

You grab it
You hate it
You want to kill it
But it is still there
Smiling at you in your face.
Smile back at it.

Fuck it. Maybe it's time to get over it…

THE STAIN OF FEMALE HUMANITY

When you say something
Cruel
You can't take it back
Away from my melting heart
Even with an
I'm sorry.

You forget
I remember
And I will recall

Cause I am a girl?

I can't zip back up
I just brew
And the stain

Remains.

I'M NOT SKINNY. I'M JUST SKINNY TODAY.

I'm not skinny. I'm just skinny today.
He had no idea that I felt my stomach curve
Around myself and
Struck the fishbone cave
Of my face
On the mirror
And knew that I was
A case by case base.

I was skinny
Today.

And not sure when
The next day of heaven
Would be.

It would
Because that's the ebb and flow
The give and take
The up and down
The nightmares of weight
It's always up
Then down
Then up
Up
Up
Then down
Deep
Then deeep.

And that's that.
Unpredictable. Unwary. Unknown.
If I only knew how to bottle
My skinny day.

DAISY DAISY

Daisy Daisy stopped eating
Pie
Daisy Daisy starting running
High

Daisy Daisy saw some results
So Daisy Daisy started something
Else

Daisy Daisy started eating
Late
Daisy Daisy puked off her
Plate

So Daisy Daisy lost all the weight
That ended up stopping her
Heart rate.

CHAPTER THREE: WOMEN

THE VAGINA

It's a deep indulgence inside your skins beneath
If it had a voice it would not cry
Or beg
It would softly say please
Now
Please now
Fuck the shit out of me.

CONDOM KILLER

What kind of person
Loses a condom
In their vagina
And says
Well, it's not going anywhere. Let's finish sex.

Then loses another one.

I THINK YOU RUINED MY VAGINA

I think you ruined my vagina
Yeah you
With your big prize
Dick.

Now when I masturbate
My veeg feels big
Bigger than before I met you
Ruined.

Hopefully not
Beyond repair.

Does the vagina ever grow back?

HABANERO BJ

i burned your dick across the tip after chopping
a pepper
and then thereafter ..
i was jacking along while licking you strong
and fingers glazed
across
the maze
of making sex its oral best
but left the haze of spicy seeds across your needs.

HORNEY

Horney
Horney
Donkey dick

Wants a piece
Of the clit
Down beneath

The nips and licks

It takes it home

Beside the groin

A whirlwind inside

Pumps me dry.

FOR ONCE

For once

For once.

You put your hand down to my warmness

And played around

Unknown penetrating feelings hit your idea of what your idea should be

I moaned a tad

To me

And give me something now wild horses

And he thrust himself into my back

My sides

My stomach.

There are fine never moments in time when you

Are fucking and there are pulsating pleasures of ah..oh heavy..fuss.

All of it

And at the end of the day

Your dick moving in the sex

Was amazing.

Trust amazing.

SEX WITH A BIG DICK

Walking soar
Your insides
Shrek to the
Outside
Of
Your lips.

Careful baby
You're blasting
My hole.

THE DAY AFTER OUR SEX

My vagina keeps excreting juice
From nowhere
Smells like an old rubber
Feels like warm happiness.

I NEED SEX

I need sex
It randomly came to me
I need to be fucked
So hard
That my hole aches
For a thrusting
Pump.

I need to be fucked
For my body's sake
And for once
My mind is not involved.

IT SMELLS LIKE PEACHES

It smells like peaches that sat in sauce
And a creamy frosting
Without the cream.

But it's always creaming.

It smells warm and fruity
Like the inside nectar of a peach
Before you hit the pit
It's that good.

Dipping the fingers in the mesh of plenty
Must be like a softness
Like no other
Better than fresh sheets on a Sunday
Satin in the back of your nightgown
Mixed with marshmallows dipping in the sun
Soft and plentiful
And the smell on your fingertips
Is sweet deep heaven.

HAVE YOU EVER LICKED MY KNEECAP?

I woke up today
Or two weeks ago... Started to rise
From the death
Of
Bullshit.
I've licked your toes
Kissed your back
Creeped my fingertips
Across the flesh
Of your
Tingling skin
And you..?

Sat simply.

NON FUNCTIONAL

And I move my mouth
Across your face
To see if you'll clutch
On
To
My lip.
My sensitive lip
Needs to be kissed
Or else…

How long do women stay in relationships with men
That don't kiss them
Much.
It's sad
Stupid
Tired

And Non-functional.

THE INSIDES

There is a heart
That sits steady
Beating hard
Deep inside
Your flesh
And that flesh tells a secret
You are strong
Hard
Capable
Renewable
You can over come
Lost love
Lost self
Lost of anything and everything
Cause you can always get back there
To the insides
Before the pain
Again
And again
And forever again.

WITH YOU WITH ME

Today I walked my heart

Down the street

With you

Tomorrow I'll walk alone

Down the street

With myself

And I hope I can
Forget that
Time with you
And go back to easy alone

Alone is easy when you

Have no distractions

With you it's hard

When you have no idea...

Are you gonna end the alone

Enough
To be

With me?

FAILURE TO LEARN THE FIRST TIME AROUND

Not only have I lost a condom
Twice
During sex
Up my vagina.

That my gynecologist had to pull out
After multiple failed attempts
On my own.

I get a bladder infection
And am not supposed to have sex
For health reasons
But
I have sex anyway.

I need to start respecting my lady
She only comes around once.

WITHOUT A YOU

Why
Don't you
Want me?
Cause I
Want you?
The chase
Falls short
The mission runs dry.
Cause I made it easy?
I want you
You want yourself

Without a me.

UNTIL YOU WALKED IN

My heart was full
With just me
It pounded alone
Feeling at home
Until you walked in.

And I tried to pretend
That I can be strong
And remain on my own
All alone
But now it's too late
My hearts starting to break
And the "I" becomes we
And the "me" becomes us
And over and over
I fall deeper

In trust.

WHO SAYS IT FIRST

I wander between
Saying
I love you
Or silencing
My heart.
Before it jumps out of my mouth
And spills all over the bed.
And I am the first one
To say it.
And roll the dice
Inside my blood
That opens my heart

To no reply.

WAX

I've never been waxed
Down there
I told myself one day
I would do it
But not just for some guy
Who likes it
You are not just some guy
Who wants it
You are a man
Who will get it
So I'll pull out all the long standing hairs

And make way for some more stares.

SO...

So...
We're friends
Who are fucking
We're fucking
Like we're friends
Can friends just be fucking?

Or is this all pretend.

MY LOVE IS LIKE A FOREIGN RAIN

My love is like a foreign rain
A pocket
Without a pen
A tear
Without a tissue.

If you loved me back I'd have...
A pleasant homemade shower
A peaceful pocket poem
A smile with some cheer
But there's no two way street here...

SLEEPING TOGETHER ALONE

Your backs to me
When we sleep
Together
Alone.
Do you not want me
In your bed?
Cause I can sleep
Better
Knowing
You don't want me
Together
In your bed.
And knowing you want me
Alone

In mine.

SIMPLY PUT

Running high
No goodbye
Simply put

You left me.

BUSY

I'm busy
Please
No need
To ring
Your silence waits
For me to break
Frustrations strong
So I'll be gone
And leave you alone
So I'll go home
Before I cry
I say goodbye.

HOW TO MAKE HIM JUST NOT THAT INTO YOU

Call him
A lot
Stalk him
Sometimes
Women
We're not psychotic

We're just really into you

And we'll do all the

Stupid shit

That women do
And
End up
Making him

Just not that into you.

TEXT ME TO THE MOON

How are you?
Busy. How are you?

So...busy as you're blowing me off?

And how are you is
I'm not trying to be a dick?

How are you?
Awesome!!
Ah..great
Two exclamation points
Does that mean you're happy to hear from me?

Or thanks for asking!! Later! Next!

There's really no pick up response to those two

Exclamation points
Got it
See ya..

Till the next text...
And let's not forget the
BEEP
And you grab that phone
To see is it him? Fuck.

It's my best friend.

Text me to the moon.

And every word
In every text
And the time it takes to get a response

Cripples the self preservation

And mental independence
So you might as well pick apart

The letters
The placement of words
On a digital screen
Cause things can be said

Different ways
Out of the mouth

And you can't tell
In a text

Text me to the moon

How are you?
I'm ok..
Do those two dots mean you're open to a conversation?

And you want a reply?

Cause….. I DON'T KNOW!!!!

IS HE TALKING TO MY LIPS?

There's a look in his eye
When he draws it to
My mouth.

A day after sex
For the first time
With a friend
And you
Try
To be friends
The next morning.

The eye drops
Down
In a conversation
To my lips
Then back up again.

Does that mean he likes me?
Something so minors going to
Torpedo my soul
While I try to figure out
What the fuck?
What's going on?
Why'd we fuck?
Gesture.

Why is he talking to my lips?
Is that a look of a telling tale?

Is it even a look?

TEAR

And a silent tear
Finds your face
And slides
Down
Slow
Like an old ice cream cone
When you talk to your best friend
About the man you love
That you haven't admitted you do
To yourself
Yet.

But that tear tells you all the answers
To the complex story.

You do love him
And he probably doesn't love you.

Tear

And the tear becomes someone you take to
remind you you are alone in this feat and will find
a way to make it ok.

NO GUARANTEE

Sometimes you're living your life
Free
Happy
Alone
Comfortable
Known
Independent
Normal
Easy.
Then you meet someone
And then you're
Heart beats
Gentle
Off balance
Scared
Opened Up.

And you run.

Cause at least there are some guarantees you'll go back to being independent. Versus ending up opened up with no guarantee.

SEX SLEEPING NEXT TO YOU

I was salivating
At the mouth
With the thought of sex
Being a breath take
Away
Right beside me

I truly wanted
To fuck
Capitol F
Fuck the fact that
You have a girlfriend
Fuck that.,
We're not doing it.

Salivating out the
Tips of my ivory stack
Tongue thirsty
For hot bloody
Sex
With carnivorous love
Beating now.

Like a misogynistic
Hungry virgin.

HE SAID I WAS A GREAT LOVER

He said I was a great lover
After avoiding my mouth
During our
Make out before you have it
Sex.

Up and down his body with my lovefull tongue
And an awkward pull away
From his side my side mouth
Not sure
Not wanting
Not knowing much
Or how.

To love.

Some can't hold intimacy
Long enough
Or enough at all
To understand it

and I want to.

EVENTUALLY

I laid in bed
And grabbed his dick
It was hard

And he said
Are you afraid it's gonna leave?

And I said
You will eventually.

Poem: 8:17

I stream of water doesn't change ones
Thoughts
Never dies a flip of a cell phone to read
Nothing.
You sit
And wait
He gets off at 8
Turns to 8:17
And than what
Do you send a text of….
God forbid
Pick up your phone
And dial
Only to get his message
And take time to record
And rerecord a message
At 8 something

Then it's 9
And you're deep in your bottle of wine
Wondering if you should do something
Make food
Go out
Open another bottle
And so call
And leave a message

Then nothing.

Nothing from a man
You slept with
Last weekend

That you think you could have liked.

THE BREAK-UP

A break up hurts
When you don't
Stick to it.

Your logic
Loses its freedom

Your independence
Has no voice

You're back where you were
Before you made the break

But worse

Cause breaking up
Wasn't enough

For you to stay away
And truly
Be broken.

So you do all the break up things

Listen to pink floyd
Or whoever

Dance in your apartment
Or whatever

Fold your laundry
Or not.

And then you have a break up

In your apartment.

OVERNIGHT

And you de-friended me on Facebook

We spent years together
As friends
Then lovers
Then a true relationship
That was met with love
That was going forward
Then went south

And now I'm nothing

And you de-friended me on Facebook

Overnight
You become de-friended.

COMPLICATED

And life gets complicated

And you don't have children
Or a husband
To fall back on
It's hard
Complicated

But maybe the word

Complicated

Is yet to be known
Or understood

Maybe we all have a meaning for it.

It's complicated to be in love with someone and not sure what's going on
It's complicated I don't have a quarter to go to the bathroom at a fast food joint
It's complicated that I'm a modern woman
It's complicated not to be interested in being taking care of
It's complicated to consistently fight against it
It's complicated when I read your text messages and know you might be cheating
Well, you have been
Like that should be enough
Yeah
It should but somehow

It's not

It's complicated when complication becomes your norm

When complications becomes accepted.

Don't let complications stir you away from yourself.

I WANTED

I just wanted a bite of your magic
I wanted your mouth in my face
I wanted you to touch my limbs

I wanted to dance in front of you
And see my fingers tickle the air.

I wanted you to lick my kneecaps
My hair
The outside of my heart

Cause I knew you weren't
Inside my love
But you were in mine.

I wanted things I couldn't have
That's why they call it wanted

Wanting never wins
It's just a terrible word people use to
Send a signal for something they can't get.

Wanting burning in lust
Gets you

Nowhere.

OH AND AH

I thought my
Ah and oh
During sex
Which were fake
Were original ah and oh
From a guy
Well they're not
Or are they?
When I have sex with different guys
They both do the
Oh..ah..
The same way as each other.
Girls fake it similarly
But we don't have
Immediate gratification
Of seeing sperm
But they do
So does that make their oh and ah
Real?
Maybe they were thinking of someone else
While they were fucking you.
Maybe their oh and ah
Was part of an imagination
I don't think I oh and ah
In my mind over another man
I think I just do it
Cause it makes it easier
Then not
So…bottom line question is
Girls can fake it

Guys can't
So when a girl fakes
Her mind is someplace else
When guys fake it to make it
It might just be
Someone else.

HALF A HEART

Half a heart feels at home
Till half a heart
Breaks the mold

Now your heart is sharing space
With someone else that
Found its place

Inside the heart beats together
With two lovers swimming
In forever….

THE GARDEN OF EDEN

And love beats at your back
Inside your heart
Beside your soul

Then eats
Your mind
Your body
Your rationality

And bad love
Becomes you
And you become it

And it tears at your
Heart
Your mind
Your soul
Your being

Your well being
And there is no
Compromise

To the darkness of the

Garden of Eden.

THE ENDING CAN'T BE GOOD

You don't want the rest of your life
To live in an a
Bipolar relationship.

But you can't help yourself
From calling
Or texting
Or writing something that is outside of
A break up

He writes
Love you
And you get upset cause he didn't say
I love you.

Then you find yourself in a see saw relationship
Which is impossible to swim through.

When you don't pick a side of the coin
And flip it up again and again
To suit your immediate desperate needs
Whether it be
Love
Affection
Knowing you're still there
In his mind
And you want him out of your mind.

Somehow you can't seem to let go
So don't.
The ending can't be good.

DON'T BE YOUR OWN PROBLEM
LONG TERM INFIDELITY

There is no way to describe the feeling you get
when you get the last evidence

After a truck load of what the fuck becomes
No longer a clue

When you get that last evidence of infidelity
And feel nothing
No sadness
No anger
No passion

You're just sterile.

You wonder how you've become that person
Or have become bogged down so many times
That you read a sad cheating email

And feel nothing.

At the very least, you'd hope you'd be pissed ,or cry, or feel
But you don't.

And then

I am thankful.

I've come to realize, holding back your truth kills.
Without honesty, you die, not softly by the way,
terribly.

OUT OF HABIT

Where does that leave us?
You still call me your girlfriend
And I don't ask you
Why do you still call me your girlfriend?
"Out of habit."
He says.
Shit. It hurts.
And you think cause he means it
Or somehow it means, it means
It's not over
Cause it's
"Out of habit."
And you stop kissing on the mouth at your greet
And get a kiss on the cheek
That non-kiss says it all.
You can call me your girlfriend out of
"Habit"
But you can kiss my ass
If you're going to say that.
Use that cushion
That I don't sit on
Or an idea
I don't lean on
Yet you use it.
And I am left
Voiceless
By choice
Cause
I don't want to hear the word
Friend

I don't want to hear the truth
I don't want to admit it's over.
So I sit in denial
In reluctancey

Of the truth.

NEVER TALK TO ME AGAIN…?

So you say I'll never talk to you again
And you say
Delete me from your phone
Trash all the poetry
I wrote you
Forget I exist
Cause you are dead to me

And weeks later you shoot
An unwanted email
Describing
Your tears
Your fears
Your love
Your need
For help

A response.

And get nothing.

Well, you asked for it
So now
You can
Drown in it.

"Is it that much easier to hate me, than to love me?...
at least I know you'll never have apathy, just yet."

Just yet.

It's fun to read past work
And still be roped
To words
That spring into
Crisp thought.
You may decide to just yet like me
Enough to call
Or think of me
In between thoughts
Across a grocery store line metal screen
Not quite sure what makes
The beep
With a laser light
Count your produce on a scale to make it total something
You always paid for my salad
And now
Whatever crossed the belt of loneliness
When I tried to hold loneliness in
So I wouldn't remember
Walking through a line
Now swiping my own card
It's that simple that it's that hard
And terrible
The no questions asked

"Are you two together cause you come here every night?"

When I swipe my card

To my own financial destination

That recalls a blind fog

Of him swiping his own card

For me

Is now apparent

When I walk through a grocery line

And pull out my card

Inside my money clip

And do it myself.

NO NO NO NO NO

No no no no no
Please don't be that person
You were
When you knew him
When he comes back

Now.

And you have a chance
To be
That person
He wanted you to be
Then
In order for him
To be with you

Now.

Quiet
Calm
Not
That
Old you
But
Now still…

You.

BROKEN

What it really feels like

A horse stomped on your chest
A lost smile
Leaves your bed
A deep breath that you can't get
Or know enough to get
Sits inside
Sequestered
Alone
Dying.

THE GENEOLOGY OF DICKHEADS

Am I supposed to forgive him

It was a mishap
A moment of stupidity

Or

A chosen act
That had every relaxation to
Doing it.

You fucked her you motherfucker

So now what?

Acting is done with a brain that fuels action and a moral chord that keeps it on track

When the moral chord loses we are left with

Tall dicks with their stupid shit.

GAMES

What if I never called him again.

And see how long it takes
To feel the feeling that I

Don't know
If you'll call me.

I have no words to describe cause
I don't know.

Why not calling him
Makes him call me.

Do I have to play:

Sorry
Shoots and Ladders
Parcheesi
Connect the dots
Memory
Risk

Do I have to play
Battle ship down
And not call you

To see

If you'll call me?!

NON-UNDERSTANDING AKA OR KNOW SHIT TO BEING WITH

I don't understand
I don't understand how
I don't
Understand

Why I'm wasting my time
My energy
My fucking life

Living in his
With him
With you
But you're lost

Not cause you spend all your time
With him
But because

You spend all your time with a man
That doesn't want you

Or know shit to begin with.

Love

It sows itself in so many dimensions.

In a pass of oxygen between a conversation.
In a soft leaf of an arm on the side of a rough soul.
It's so easy to justify
Why he's not…

There in
Love
With you

What?
Why?
How?
You can never change the brain or heart that sells
itself to

Love.

I CRY ON MY SLEEVE

I cry on my sleeve
Not cause you hurt me
Cause I hurt myself.

And I don't know why
I fall into
My trap
Over and over
Again.

What is my trap
Other than pain
Loss
Hurt.

Why do I bleed unconditionally
From my heart

In a trap that I made.

And think about all the time I lost
Loving you

And all the time I have
To hate myself

For it.

DAISIES

I call him
I call him not.

I call him
I call him not.

Wait

Maybe I'll just
Text him.

Right?

MARIJUANA BLOW JOB PIPE

You know it's bad when
You're smoking pot out of
Your pipe
And start
Sucking it like it's a
Dick

I need dick.

THE INFINIITY PHONE STICK

I'm not a piñata
At your party

Beating me down with your infinity phone stick.

Stop riffling out your
Phone

In the middle of
Talking to my parents
Watching a movie
Standing still
Running a light
Sitting up
Lying down
Eating fries
Walking home

Stop the infinity phone stick

Anything
Everything.

Stop being a phone prick
That fell into
The phone age

You're not that important
And a sort of kind
That's
Alone.

SCREWED

If I could change my brain
I could change my life

Of memories
Of you

But I can't
So I won't

Which means

I'm left

SCREWED

Into the floor
Of permanency

How do I pull myself out
Of

Your bolt?

How do you unscrew

Your – SELF

To become the self

GIRLFRIEND

We talked about how amazing our sex is
We talked about me going on the pill
We talked about our childhoods
We talked about our fears and tears
    And hopes
        And dreams.

But we never talked about being together
We never talked about making it official
We never talked about you
    Calling me
        Your girlfriend.

How is it possible to talk about everything
And not talk about that?
And not say those bedrock words:

I want you

    To be

        My girlfriend.

WHEN YOU LIKE HIM

every fucking word
gets collapsed
ripped apart
torn to pieces
every detail
every gesture
is played out
over and over and over again
inside your head
locked swirling
between memories of your time together
that attack your brain
with no control of stopping it

when you like him.

AT SOME POINT

At some point
Obviously at some point

You hope
To forget

That there was

Love.

CORPORATION SEX

We had corporation sex
Like a missionary engine
Waiting for the
Pump to fill the hole

Of bodies together
Like a habit
Which should be hung
Like a jury that
Has one person say no

Well, I say no
I'm the hung jury
Wanting non-corporation sex.

Corporations
Probably hate jury duty
They hate the whole system
Cause it might unveil things they're not ready to expose

But in bed
I don't want to be corporation sex.

ANYWHERE OTHER THEN HERE

I wanna get in there
The quick kiss and leave you outside the door
Before I get a chance to feel your lips

I wanna get your flesh to collapse
And let me breath into it

I want you to pick up your tongue and shove it
into my mouth
Be vulnerable
Be tired
Be insecure
Be something

Other than me trying all the time
To get you there
There..

Anywhere other than here.

SHOULD YOU TRY IT

It's not like the most beautiful thing
When it is the scariest thing
To be thrown into
Love
Hot desperate passion
Open eyes into the torpedoes of someone's heart
Like a gaze you can't hold
Or a smile you seep beneath your careful throat.

Girl finds boy
Guy meets girl
She crashes hard
Against the surface of
Desert cracks
Found after a long coming rain
Waiting alone
Leaving her more
Alone
When the regular
Sun
Comes up
And the rain drains beneath the cracks
And that is that.

Girl meets boy
Girl falls onto hard clayed
Cold terrain
And the boy goes away.

BEFORE

I think I tell the truth across my pencil page
But then I read something from before
From before I lost your feelings deep inside my holes
Before I woke up one day and was a little better
Before was before
And you don't recall that time
Before.
Cause it bled so hard in the ears
And ripped down your side
While flurrying your mind with blank nothingless love
That you spray on my heart
Every day
Praying that one day
It will be before.
Before I loved you
Before I felt like red gems glistening in a thin lake
You wonder where it happened

That I got over you.

THE HATED LEWBOWSKI

When you become a
"Yeah man"
Or a
"Dude"

With a guy.

You better just
Hang your
Sexuality

On the rim of your beer.

Dude…Man.

No motherfucker
I'm a Woman, DUDE!

Not Lewbowski.

CHAPTER FOUR: THE CITY

ON SUNSET BLVD.

A red Mercedes pulls out onto Sunset
Cars wait at a red light
By the old Tower Records
Next to the new Coffee Bean.

The movie billboard
Above the Bean
Stands fierce
A foot space away
On the pedal
Before the next same billboard
Hits your eye
Above the viper room.

A GMC truck
An orange street cleaning car
And an Atlantic express
Shuffle down the crippled highway
Of Sunset Blvd.

A cool breeze in a warm sun
Must be like the drive
Thru and thru
Down the strip
Of changing cars.

A man with a handkerchief
Wrapped around his head
For a hat
Sits outside a bar

As yellow turns to red.

"The light is very shiny
It's almost clear sometimes.
I like a rainy day."
He plays with his visor
In his fat fingers
As the sun beats down over each car

Swirling by the coast.

MAN BROWN BAGGING IT ON SKID ROW

Drink
Drink
Drink it
Down

Without a home
Walking the streets
Of sin
Beaming in some gin

This is his home
A part of skid row
Nothing else
To know

While he boozes
His way
Along a way
To his tent

Which is home.

Downtown LA

The heat of the streets
The homeless whores
In my hometown
The heart of LA
Is only found

In downtown.

GOD BLESS THE ICE CREAM TRUCK

I love the ice cream trucks
That sit on corners
Throughout New York City
In the humid hot summer
I go to the one on Prince and Broadway
It sits there all day
Hitting up the tourists
With their shopping bags
And thirsty smiles
Licking up all the excitement
Polished off with a chocolate cone
Dipped in rainbow sprinkles
The tired owner of the bus
Hangs over the steering wheel
With his sumo forearms
Resting on the wheel
As he holds up a box radio
He pulls it closer
The chord stretch out
From the socket
And the game plays on
While a Russian woman blasts
Cone after cone
Through the window
Enticing passing people torched
By the sun
On the congested streets
One can't help but notice
The childlike customers
Licking drips of heaven
Around their cool cone
And you step up to get one
The mystery sealed with a summer kiss.

WASHINGTON SQUARE PARK

The fountain springs high out of the ground
Like a fire hydrant undone
In the middle of the park.

An Indian walks his bike
Repeatedly ringing its bell
Mumbling incoherent tones.

An Asian girl softly walks up to a student
And hands out a pamphlet
As she highlights her reader
Their eyes never meet
The Asian eyes drop as
The readers head dives forward
In the text
Hiding behind her work to avoid
Saying no.

A woman chatting on the phone
Drops her plastic bag
And tells her friend
She just dropped her dinner.

A four feet something kid
Practices his skateboarding moves
In front of the benches
Of watchful eyes glazed over in a trance
Of the shooting flames.
The fountain.

A constant force
In the park
A center with a steady flow in the ever changing
stories
Transpiring across the cement.

In Washington Square park.

THE KNOWN BENEATH YOUR SHOE

The trampling on the street
The dirty hair
Met with the buses stench

The city
Your neighborhood

Known and unknown
Places
On a block
That you or I walk down

Whether it's unknown or known

It's still a street in the city you reside in

And your feet stride the pavement
Fitting in

Cause it's the ground that makes the world around us

Be together.

5 am WALK IN A CUBOARD WORLD

Sometimes you wake up
In a place
You know
In a haze
From the night
Before.

And you walk down
The steep of the Hollywood hills
Carrying your stubborn
Heels.

Caused there's not a taxi outside a mansion
In the a world where Porsches run like water
Down fountains
In the pool.

It's a very very cupboard world.

ORANGE MOON

The moon sits wild
In an orange shield
With its usual gray doubts
Upon the surface.

Slowly risen above a building
Hanging in
Mid air
Staring me down.

Straight
Ready
Loving
Wanting

It's your moon.

It's your night.

And the moon dives deep
And the heart dies slow

And the rest of the world

Sits
Quietly.

IT'S GREEN

KFC
Carl's Jr.
And
The Green Burrito.

A triple threat
On 7th Avenue
Stacked on top of each other
Like an angry come beef me now
Food court.

As the signage
Peels out onto
The street
For….

Do you have any change?
A bum paces the trio
For what….

Mashed potatoes
At bowtie Granpa's barn
The shithole burger
At the Starship
Or
A green burrito.

A green burrito?
It's green.

Which would you pick given no change?

Will work for change.

Will die of a heart attack.

I SEE THE LIGHTS FLICKER

I see the red lights flicker
Outside my window

It's the fire station
In the depth of
Skid Row

It's a busy station
Row is unlike anywhere else
In this world
It's a city of hard
Chronic
Get out of my face
People.

Yet, I sit and watch the lights getting ready
To bleed into the night
And hit up the next war
The next crap feast
The next thing that is horrible

And the bleed goes on
Throughout the night
But it's the nights
I like to observe
When I sit at my desk

Cause it goes off all the time
And every time
It reminds me of badness

It keeps it calling
In the rain
In the frames of humanity
On the streets

And I'm still not surprised
By the light
By the roaring sound
But still
It's surprising to occur

That much.

SUNSET AT 6:22 PM IN DOWNTOWN LOS ANGELES

The sun slides down
From the bottom of the buildings

To the top.

Orange scent hits the imagination
And the backdrop of
Smog
Is
Velvet glaze
Burrowing to the top

Of the atmosphere.

And makes it rich

In color.

www.ingramcontent.com/pod-product-compliance
Lightning Source LLC
Chambersburg PA
CBHW020938090426
42736CB00010B/1180